Trumbull Ave.

Made in Michigan Writers Series

General Editors

Michael Delp, Interlochen Center for the Arts
M. L. Liebler, Wayne State University

Advisory Editors

Melba Joyce Boyd
Wayne State University

Stuart Dybek
Western Michigan University

Kathleen Glynn

Jerry Herron
Wayne State University

Laura Kasischke
University of Michigan

Thomas Lynch

Frank Rashid
Marygrove College

Doug Stanton

Keith Taylor
University of Michigan

A complete listing of the books in this series
can be found online at wsupress.wayne.edu

Trumbull Ave.

Poems by Michael Lauchlan

Wayne State University Press
Detroit

ISBN 978-0-8143-4096-7 (paperback)
ISBN 978-0-8143-4097-4 (e-book)

Library of Congress Control Number: 2014946150

∞

Publication of this book was made possible by a generous gift from
The Meijer Foundation. Additional support was provided by Michigan
Council for Arts and Cultural Affairs and National Endowment for the Arts.

Designed and typeset by Bryce Schimanski
Composed in Interstate and Dante

For the kids—all of them

Contents

CONTENTS

CONTENTS

John Worthington (Photo by author)

Acknowledgments

Many thanks to John Freeman and Martha Carlson Bradley for continual collegial criticism and support as well as manuscript review. Thanks to Tom Lux, who has been a wise mentor since 1979. Thanks to Joan Aleshire and Pam Harrison, for enduring earlier versions. Thanks also to significant support from friends Helen Fremont, Ken Grunow, Geraldine Grunow, M. L. Leibler, Lou Baltman, Dan Minock, Rick Clancy, Mark Bauer, and Jim Michels. This collection of poems could not have taken its present shape without the brilliant and patient work of Annie Martin. As an effort spanning decades, these poems would be inconceivable without the loving support of Deborah McEvoy and our fabulous kids.

Poems in this volume have been included in the following publications: *Apple Valley Review, Blood Orange, Boxcar, Chiron Review, Collagist, Cortland Review, Crab Creek Review, Driftwood, English Journal, I-70, Innisfree, New England Review, Nimrod, November 3rd Club, Peninsula Poets, Poetry Quarterly, San Pedro Review, Slipstream, Tampa Review, Third Wednesday, Thrush, The Tower Journal, Victory Park, Virginia Quarterly Review.*

"Elm," Liturgy on Trumbull," "Water Heater, 18th St.," "1943," "Hospital Cafeteria," "Dad and I, in a Snap," and "Sunday Morning, 1993" were included in Sudden Parade, from Ridgeway Press, 1997.

Trumbull Ave., 1981

The bounding dog may have been a Dane.
Memory does not retain the breed, save
that his large frame bulged with muscles
and he ran with the happy grace of athletes
beyond praise and blame and score. The sun
hammered that broad anvil of Detroit—
the squinting hookers; the wan wild kids
up from Tennessee; black kids one step
from Alabama; the old Armenian
who ran the cleaners, who still wept
for dead parents and his young bride
seventy years after. As for me—strange
to waken each day into the same life,
or, now, into the sequel of the story—
I stood, half blind from cooked
concrete and flashing windshields,
near the burned apartment where a kid
had been killed and others sniffed or
shot or swallowed whatever they could
and fell into some drastic sleep. The dog
came from a side street chasing a mate
or just running from sheer canine joy—
the old Ford invisible to him as
God's fist. Poised on the ruined hood,
a most sudden sculpture, he died fast.

Slab

Screeding the wet cement, dragging a board
over the forms, he works the gray mass flat,
then, with the wood float, rubs the stones
deep into the slab, letting the smooth grains
rise to the surface. Later, he'll smooth it
with a magnesium, then broom it
and pour a potion of curing fluid.
He straightens to rinse the lime
from his gloves and pants, to wash
the chalky residue from the drive, to let
his back release its knot of pain.
A small boy is practicing the crossover
as he walks to the schoolyard court,
the ball slapping against the echoing street.
A woman shouts into a phone, tires wail,
and from a world gone quiet, traffic
asserts its buzz of engines, brakes,
lawn mowers, and the familiar "pop—
pop—pop" where talk has broken off.

Water Heater, 18th St.

In a half cellar, dim, with a dirt floor
wet from sewage and a bad water heater,
one smell, sharper than the rest,
wrinkles the nose of the plumber.
Teeth grind, the scalp tingles—
he waves a pipe wrench at the frozen rat
and steps boldly again. Pipes cut, he
drags the old heater up the block steps to the alley
while the sun drops behind charred row houses,
their walls opened, staircases, banisters
leading to rose-papered sleeping rooms.
Two men stop him, offer sockets,
ladders, drills—cheap. Silent,
he removes a pipe from the heater, then
turns on them, cursing through his teeth.
They run, sliding in the icy alley,
shouting, "Crazy son of a bitch,"
and vanish behind the row houses.
He leans the heater against the dumpster,
grips the rusty bottom, and heaves it in.

Milk, 1933

When the gas man came for your meter,
your oldest let him in. You jumped
from your chair and handed him the baby—
"Take her, too! How will I feed her
if I can't warm the milk?" After he fled,
you were ashamed. You were nursing,
of course, and had never lied to a soul.
Five decades later you still see him,
nearly as hungry as you, his wrench
in one hand and, from the other,
your quiet Ellie gaping up.

Bread, 1933

Widowed with eight kids, how young
you were in a cold flat in a strange town.
On the porch, your youngest wept
until you could ladle some vague stew
for dinner. When a strange, silent man
saw him and dropped off a bag
of flour, you scrounged yeast and salt,
followed like a recipe an old image—
your mother baking in a farm kitchen
in Manitoba. White motes hung
in the air as you mixed and laughed,
kids swirling, the oven belting its heat
as the leavened loaves rose, then
baked brown, and, for once, fed all.

Glove

From what we cannot hold the stars are made.
        W. S. Merwin

The hand fits it, slips
into the dark imprints
of use. Above the web,
leather is scuffed by years
of infield dirt. You wear it
loose and let it snap around
the ball, catching your son's
sharp toss again and again.
When he sails one,
you can't leap but flick
your wrist to let the glove
hawk into the air.

He will take it south
with him and write to you
of *béisbol* with sugarcane
cutters and banana men,
of the heat and the hops,
and a squat one-armed ump.
When he falls into a river
to snare a drifting foul,
the ump's hand will jump.
In the dusk of that field
ground rules lapse and
no ball falls out of play.

The Color of Our Kitchen at Dusk

When anyone passing might look in
and catch us half-dressed, enflanneled,
you find in your laptop timeslots
for the patient who wept to you today
about her spent daughter, about all

that was already wrong before cancer.
From drowsing over student work, I rise
to wash dishes but pause instead to stroke
your hair as you click your patient
into the hours of her future days.

Then you call her as the yellow deepens
toward a shade which slides under us
like the sound of an old fiddle filling a hall
where everyone draws breath from one well
and drinks one sound together without shame.

In the burnt-sky kitchen, you fix everything
and nothing for a woman you haven't seen yet,
for a voice which will prod you awake
when the house is gray, when no one passes
and no trembling note fills the night.

Hospital Cafeteria

Opposite me, young nurses chat,
holding wheat toast in delicate hands.
One has just shaved an old man
and claims she made him laugh.
Even as you read this he is gone
and maybe the nurses and I, as well, because you,
dear one, are the slowest correspondent.
Once, I found a letter I'd set aside to type
eight years earlier (on your scale
a fingernail of time, a twitch):
scrawled details of my pregnant wife and sick friend.
I've long since built his casket,
which was a joke between us: "How's it coming?
Better hurry." "It's gorgeous. Don't rush me."
Every night my son bounces a ball on the steps
until windows rattle. When the "barber"
and her pals head back to their floor,
she speaks of tiling her kitchen.
The gift shop volunteer who sold me
a begonia steers her walker toward my table.
Think of the Series stopped by an earthquake.
What an odd place to put a ballpark, this earth,
her plates' slow fluidity dwarfing us
as we scramble home from second on a hit.

Mementos

Leaves flip over as light
razors into dark. Flies bite.
Birds scrounge for bugs.
A door bangs. We shift
weight from foot to foot,
thinking, *What next?* and
trying to sort out why
the popping of rain on dirt
recalls fire, why fire evokes
the city blowing apart but
also us, decades back, kissing
in a downpour, your face
bright and wet, or why love
and riot awaken a kitchen
on a bacon-frying Sunday
before Dad died. *Rain,*
newsmen said, rolling six
lies into one, *ended the riot,*
though the charred remains
of housefires still stink like
a wet dog sneaking in just
before lightning's next burst.

1943

When he gets off the Baker at Woodward,
from the west side come white boys with tire-irons;
black gangs on the east want him to join.
He snakes and dodges like a tired fighter.
Finally home and his boy starts in on him,
saying that he's a man now
(really fourteen but he looks grown),
saying Ma agrees he can go.
When the boy starts crying, he can't stand it
and signs the army's paper.

Badgered past confusion,
this hungry welder sits at a kitchen table
smelling chicken and tasting a quiet
he had wanted as if it were peace.
My memory would hold him here
with his wife turning the chicken,
his only child turning the radio dial
for the last time.

Misty Night with Dead Ford

Walk past a stilled construction site,
gravel heaped beyond a steel fence,
to chat with your mechanic
about the life your wheezing truck
might have left. He's serious yet
hopeful, wiping his hands on a rag
and getting a breath between cars
in the lot outside his garage.
With names sewn onto workshirts,
doctors might look like Chris,
young and tired, trying to hold off
the inevitable on a night Poe
would use—the mist
lending street lamps a glow
as they kick on—or Hitchcock,
in flicks that chilled your young
nights but distracted you, in those
air-raid years, from the bomb
heading for a crosswalk near you.

Red Ruby

In the Red Ruby, a woman is sweeping,
an old broom resting in her fingers
like a long paintbrush.
She gathers bits of noodles, cookies,
a fortune offering lotto numbers
and "luck in love." Here,
the horse goes off with the rat
again and again as 1949
becomes 1975 and 1999.
Nixon bombs Cambodia,
is reelected and resigns
while we meet and meet again
and a woman sweeps a dark carpet
shush, shush, shush
under red chairs and tables
and we are born and born and born.

Tires

Somebody loves us all.
    Elizabeth Bishop, "Filling Station"

After my son has rolled the car
and crawled out, I go to see Mike and Paul
to replace bald tires. Their grandpa built
the shop and house on the edge of town.
Their dad met Ford during a fill-up
and has often told me from the seat
where he answers the phone and remembers.
Old tools abound, smoothed by use—
sledge, lever, vise, jack—"oil-soaked,
oil permeated . . ." Old pictures askew
on shelves show a city not yet pinched
by freeways, emptied by blight.
To ease my wait, Dad has saved
magazines since the Normandy beachhead.
One recalls Chile in that radiant season
before Pinochet and the stadium of blood.
So vivid, these young faces caught
at markets or marching under signs.
How we long for that other world,
for the past that shimmers on a page,
a future that verged on real.
A tire pops onto a rim. An air
wrench rings out in the garage.
An oily paper on the rack
carries shots from Baghdad. Here
in Detroit, my son has crawled out
of a crumpled car, and Mike and Paul
are wrestling radials onto wheel hubs
in a tire shop built before the war.

Elm

When I was a kid the elms died
by thousands. Those green cathedrals
above our streets, where a thrown ball
might glance off four branches
and still let a veteran fielder
get under it, smack the glove,
be Kaline or Colavito—
like quiet heroes, those trees are gone.

Except one. Maybe saved by dozers
when the city cleared a dozen blocks
then forgot why for twenty years.
Dutch elm skipped over one wide trunk
that spreads leaves before river winds
filled with tomatoes and alfalfa
from Ontario, sounds of freighters,
sounds of bread trucks, car haulers.

Over my wife's bare shoulder, I once
watched it draw a breath. Its slow rasp
mixed with distant thunder,
sheer curtains spreading, clothes
rustling down, and the start
of a slow, delicious rain.

She Lives Now

For Agnes

Having lost blood and ripped out the IV,
she will not wake. Gaping, she snores, slow
as the rasp of waves heard above the shore

in a late-night house. She's not the sound,
not the gape, not the restive ear still awake
in the kitchen of the house. She lives now

in the turning force that rolls water toward sand
where it will spend itself and slide back below.
For years, she has pushed breath from her throat

as though shaping the phrases of a book
from laugh lines and grief, with terse words
for the work that lay between. She will close,

breathing an almost endless passage—a surf
in storm and in breezy chop or driven rain,
then, under eggshell skies, the softest swells.

Into Silence

The seat creaks, or the frame of the bike.
Wind sucks around my helmet.

A truck blows by on a curve and
I fix my eye on the white line
of the shoulder, then for a while on
nothing but effort as the road rises.

Finches, cardinals, thrushes trill;
sparrows brawl. Then *kikuyakuyaku*
echoes in the hush. In her last year,
Mom taught my youngest bits

of Slovenian. She gave him
a warbling *kukuyoo* sound to ask,
"What's happening?" By then,
all conversation came in bursts,

clarity followed by blanks,
until the ritual of chat rebooted.
Birdlike, we called to each other,
I'm here, I'm here, still here.

Into silence, Merton said, something
always comes—tires rubbing themselves
bald against the pavement, distant traffic,
birds I can't name, my oldest fears.

And rasping from a hospital room,
my mother's last wry word.

Do Me a Favor

We lie staring up
letting our breathing slow itself,
though my heart tries
to drum its way out of me.
It seems a good time to ask
if you'd forget my worst moves.
After thirty years, you still evoke
my favorite Hemingway nurse,
who might have grown more lovely
if Ernest hadn't let her bleed out
in a Swiss maternity ward.
Like her, you lie sweetly. And
you lie beside me as I think
of hours spent fuming, nights
I've glared into the dark.
Breathing softly now,
your sweet shape shifts. Matisse,
Renoir, and a few others
have covered this, but I love
the way your hip rises
from your little waist, your legs
curling in sleep, and the way
your sleeping form recalls
what made our hearts jump.
Without you, without your soft
breathing dreams, joy slips
into a list of snits, of fears
for the icy day that, right now,
climbs across the Atlantic.
Do me a favor, I say to your shape,
when I need it, tell me a lie.

Detroit Pheasant

From a window, the boss calls to us
where we load his truck with bricks.
"Turn around fellas—look."
A pheasant wades through the brown grass
across the street, vanishing
and emerging from the tangle.
A shed leans near a phone pole.
Bumpers glint from the weeds.
Blocks from the old foundation
angle through the earth.
The pheasant paces his courtyard.

We have killed the city which lived here.
The hieroglyph of its streets and rails
has joined the ancient lost tongues.
Buds unfold on a dwarf maple.
A rooster hollers.

Haul

Hours of asphalt, orange
construction cones, trucks
coughing in the wrong lanes,
and old qualms, caffeine-laced,
flicking across the windshield—
it is, as you say, a haul.
The sky shifts over pine hills
that flatten into gleaned fields.
From the radio preacher you
slide numbly to news of a quake

that killed hundreds, to the Top
40 of 1970 and the score
of a late season game. Like
death, a dream winks from rocks
beyond the guardrails. Sultry,
the voice of a jazz DJ
seeps in from a college town
where you might have taught
had things worked out in your
imagined past. You ride
in a bubble of sound and self,
singing fragments of song,
reliving bits of love or rage,
shame or pique, each brake light
jangling you back like
alarm bells and school bells
or like nothing else, as you purr
around a real wreck glad still
to be awake and wiggling all

limbs, moving toward a bed,
grinding past mileposts and

thinking how the Romans sank
stones every thousand steps
all the way to Britain, where they
remain, like Latin grammar and
word roots, along the old bricked *via*.
As the dark hovers, you finally
settle into a rhythm as the road
throbs though wheel hubs
and springs and into your bones.

Gifts

Scrapping an old fire escape,
you tune a flame to blue. Iron
splatters into sunspots. Above,
a flange pulls loose, tumbles lethal
until a wordless boy, perched in some
high window, deflects your death
with a torn hand and a quick heart.
His face still turns upward, though

his name is gone, who salvaged
the shape of your skull. A boy his age,
when your dad died, you gulped
down your mother's spoken gift,
It will be easier now—I know,
as if she could clear her throat,
speak a word, and, from all that
wreckage, forge a man.

Today, your monumental pal
sees you walk into a party store
while three guys circle in behind.
He waits, leaning on a phone pole,
deciding which punk he'll take
first. Then you emerge, blinking,
and they split. He shrugs, says,
I just didn't like the look of them.

And his iambic line clatters in
among the echoes, thrown down
like the large first drops of rain
popping in dust after heat.

Letter to a Dead Friend

Like a deaf guy who phones,
I can't know for sure
but speak in case you'll hear.

Once you called on me to save
an old man's frozen house.
In his cellar you held a troublelight
while I changed pipe after split pipe,
staying only because the orange glare
and your gaunt smile held me.
Weeks later we buried you.

In dreams I haul crates of ash
along avenues gone serpentine,
stepping over prone men and women,
hands shoved into pockets, gray.

You deserve your vacation
in the Bahamas of Death;
but help us, you bodiless wonder,
though we carve each day a slice
of doom—yet, in the late

clack and hiss of radiators,
in the labored breath of a sick kid,
visit us—adamant, bent on blood;
guide us alleyways by troublelight.

Carolers

Your open mouths laughing, you walk
toward me, three girls with your young
mom, all grinning through me, making me
ache a bit as when I've tweaked the bad
knee and can't quite breathe, seeing you
pass flushed with song under street lamps
(as maybe never before or again), and
sorry I won't live eons with your bright
side-looks as you laugh off some old
fight—loud tears, then a wet embrace.
I would hold you all just long enough
to revive Walker Evans and let him
shove a fresh plate into his view
camera while the first flakes curl past,
but he and his unfamous women and men
are engaged with serious entropy. He'd
want to get your mother's dark eyes
searing into distance as she keeps the tune
and remembers things she never spoke,
even to you. With your long strides,
your breath-clouds and voices, how
would he ever catch you, if he rose?

Storm

With the first drops, the storm
snapped the willow, smacked a limb
to the ground, so the dog quivered
to our door with me a step behind.
My chainsaw coughed long enough
to throw the chain and send me
searching for screwdrivers, bar oil,
and rags. All year a bench collects
the vestiges of tasks like odd parts
of days. Bench therapy is crude.
I scrape nails and screws into cans
of nails and screws. Drill bits
are shelved. Pipe wrenches rejoin
the plumbing bucket. Finally,
I pry the saw's orange case
to gaze into a greasy mystery,

knowing I'll end up at the hardware,
in a line of old guys with dead saws.
A vague dread makes me try
to trust my hands. After an hour,
oiled and gassed, the saw starts
and runs rough, then steadies.
I climb a ladder to a perch
in the crotch and cut a groove
around the broad limb as my hand
goes numb and my son holds
tension on a rope to save the fence.
When I bear down it digs
through bark and green wood.
What's left of the branch falls hard,

burrows into sod softened by rain,
littered with fronds. We carve
what's left into stumps for the chipper
and lug it all to the curb,
panting and grunting as quiet
returns and the chainsaw cools.

Outside the Community Center

Behind a chop shop you rebuilt
with your daughters, a local waif,
and a young me, you might still wait
on the cement truck, the sun rising,
a level in one hand, a sledge in the other,
the shadow of a builder god.
But you're gone. One more loss
on one more job made a bullet
through your heart seem irresistible.

If I caught up with you in an alley
where you'd drop tools to chase
johns away from neighborhood girls,
what could I say that mattered
and wasn't just another lie
offered up for the dead while I
cling to my day above ground?
The cement is poured and finished.
The forms are pulled up. Around
the building, grass goes uncut
and families have mostly split,
making room for casinos and acres
of well-lit car lots. The street girls

have a shelter now, and your own
girls have raised your grandkids. You
taught me to guzzle coffee, to love
work and sweat and cool morning air,
to wait as a new sun makes its way
over the bread plant and a truck
whines into view, rolling its load
into a mix we can use.

Charlie Gabriel Bending

Not to show feeling, but to reach
and draw some gut-popping squawk
from down where it lives. Once,
I helped a plumber bump a boiler
down cellar steps. As he bent to lift
he looked at me like, Kid, I hope
you're serious. Lifting, Charlie blows
serious as the New Orleans vaults
where his people wait on resurrection
and grim as the dank parish
that sent him decades back
up the long, dark river to here.

Stairs

With a pencil sharpened on a chisel
he traces the framing square again and again—
rise 7, run 10.
Cutting, he leaves the line on the keeper side,
cleans out the corners with a handsaw,

then marks off the treads and kicks,
giving himself the simplest
hieroglyphic order:
cut here   now here   now here.

On the high porch of a courtyard, light failing,
he gathers saw, square, rasp, and power cords,
ripping hammer, and boxes of nails.
He finds his punch in the last glimmer,
hoists the box to his shoulder and starts down,

smiling faintly at the silence
of each step. Like stone, he thinks,
like a terraced mountainside
where an old couple might descend
from their third floor kitchenette
with never a creak. The wind hits,

the crate bites, and fingers go numb
as he swings onto the lowest porch.
In the burnout across the alley,
a thug might hope he makes two trips.
The left hand gropes ahead for balance,
pulling after it his slow strides,
a cord dangling in the wet snow.

Snow

What creature flails like an old man?
You find Moceri struggling, lost
in a drifted alley, and bring him home
while the blizzard blows. Small, frail,
good-humored but soft on details
and documents, he has no ID
and no idea where he lives. After soup
and dry socks, the story spills out.
Daughters grown, a son in jail,
he lives in a downtown flop.

We start into the white, silent city.
"This depression," he tells me
as I swerve through rutted streets,
"is tougher than the last. Then
you could get help. We were all
in the same crappy boat." Ice tears
at my muffler as I bounce across lanes.

When he is delivered to a sour room
behind a well-chewed door, I emerge
to blow steam into the bright gloom
and compose a story for you—
of Moceri warm and safe at home.
I'll skip the way the street curls its lip
as he passes, the way the glass shakes
in his one window as the wind
slides in. But you know already
the thin fabric of our skin,
the threadbare coat we clutch
against every winter to come.

Liturgy on Trumbull

In mid-baptism we rush from the house
to ask them to stop.
They had chased a man to the middle of this street
and were beating him.
Now he slumps near the curb while they name his crime.
I know Ronnie, the chubby guy with no shirt.
He lands one last kick on the thief's dazed face,
then backs off, cursing him loudly, demanding his "stuff."
"Go home for chrissake," his wife yells,
"or the cops'll take you." He leaves.

Ronnie's wife keeps a hand on the guy's shirtcollar,
though he never even looks up,
just leans forward now and then to spit.

Someone lights a cigarette for the thief
while we talk about the city going to hell.
On someone's radio the Tigers are winning a ballgame.

My wife crosses the street holding a napkin.
For the life of me I can't think what she's carrying.
"Body of Christ," she says.

Flossie

We've retold how, drooling blood,
tracks tattooed across her ribs,
our pup slumped in the kitchen,
only to rise when you cracked
an egg in her dish. And how, years
later, she'd follow our son
when he toddled through an open gate
toward the four-lane abyss.
By such fingers we cling
to stories and fur. You named
the dog after the stubborn infant
in *White Mule*. She trotted alongside
while you strollered the babies
downtown and back. Who grips
life like a grateful stray?
I thought I knew *desire*,
had felt it morph into some
smoky essence distilled in novels.
Awake between us, it made
us shriek delight and made me
hold you sometimes too tightly.
Now, it clicks beside us,
padding in quick rhythm, as though
nudging us past the chasm,
toward a story's own end.

Frond

Dwarfed, a man stands in a willow,
propped between limbs, holds
an idling saw, and stares at a branch
dangling just beyond his reach.

If he could speak above the growl
of a saw and owned one word
equal to his limbs' longing for rest,
if his sound reached any ear,

would he not become the tree's own
voice and merge with the green hush
until he sang only the one true
grammar of the waving frond?

Backyard Ice

I'm five, being laced into skates
by a young beauty in a long coat.
Our yard is frozen and lit up
by floodlights. I keep saying

floodlight, thinking how my brothers
have flooded the yard with hot
water to make smooth ice,
an inch at a time, hooking a hose

to our old laundry tub in the still
hours after midnight. *Floodlight*.
I shuffle in double-bladed skates
and snowpants while they fly,
turn, and stop in a spray of ice.

I can't afford to doubt
this thread of love, this trout
silvering past in a cold stream
of memory, seducing, vanishing

into the fuzz of these hours
where I worry over time,
as though it needs our help
to find its way across a clock.

Reading Herodotus

If you should dip your hand in,
your wrist would ache immediately.
        Elizabeth Bishop "At the Fishhouses"

If you meet my student and
hear the voice slip from his mouth
like gauze torn from a wound,
you'll learn of his hungry flight
from Saddam, hiding out with Mom
and brother, then fording a river
when guns held the bridge,
crossing the sand, hoping in a line

of American troops. Herodotus
himself would admire our print
accounts of kings, fools, blood,
and broken cities offered up
in lines of rising smoke
as if to ward off fate. Nearby,
in ancient sites, burnt flesh
has dried to dust, and stones
still hold transfigured grief.

The immediate ache in your bones
when you meet my student means
you're not yet deaf. If you dip
your hand into this opaque river,
no limb comes out, no skin,
no word, but one inhuman note—
the car-wreck shriek of a mother
over a boy's frail form.

Orchid

The insistent light finds the woman's bed
as it found a girl leaning on Rembrandt's half-door,
found Peter and Magdalene in Renaissance shades

of blue and ochre and, mixed on the palette,
that bit of phosphorous that could explode
on a forehead. It is November. Morning

over an alley leaks through a blind and
pours itself onto the coverlet and the red,
hip-shaped blanket. At her neck, black silk

demurs, but a shock of hair, a cheek reflect
a glow into the sleeping room where,
hungry for light, an orchid sips on air.

Sunday Morning, 1993

after Coltrane's "Alabama"

Above the Victorian window arches
of a stone facade, parapets
lean only where demo has begun.
I turn a corner, crunching snow,
truck filled with a Coltrane tune.
A gaunt lament in '63,
now it even aches for him.
Around back, the torn foundation gapes
where brickers have left off.
Someone has graffitied the firewall:
MEMORY
brushed on in white.
Bricks flare, glazed sidewalks shine,
and steam is ripped from manholes
in lucent sheets.
"If these were silent,
even the stones would cry out."
Stones weep; brick and mortar bellow like
a reed calling on God,
like a mother keening, like
four girls killed again and again,
hoping and dying among stones and song
and the vacant prayer of an empty street.

Holiday Antacid

In the pharmacy, buying antacids,
I wait behind a small gray woman
as she writes a check with a palsied hand.
I shuffle, survey shelves of talking
Santas, green plates, and placemat tableaus
where even the wise men seem American.
I can, if I like (and who wouldn't)
check my colorectal status
or buy a Fleets. I consider my need
for an accurate digital scale and
have almost chosen reading glasses
when my tremulous neighbor lifts
her parcels and compliments the hair
(now auburn) of the cashier. Moments later
I hold the door for her and we leave
the store together, entering the slush
of suburbia, sliding slowly toward
the thrum of traffic at the crosswalk,
toward the ice-filled gutter.

Inconsolable

The woman in your old house recalls
your grandmother, who died in 1953,
though your own kids now have kids,
though this slight, bent woman speaks
no Slovenian, and doesn't know you.

Do you know you? Your father sifts
through your face, your temper. When
you laugh, your mother pours out
from lips, breath, syllables, cells.
Over time, the house has shifted and

she struggles walking. So, order lumber.
Cut wedge-shaped joists and level the floor.
Jacking floor joists would just make
trouble for her. Do you want to replaster
as well? It's not about the house.

Prevent her stumbling. She's Grandmother.
The Fox knew this, and the Potawatomi:
we arrive, copulate, get born, and die,
but we never leave. The faces that look
familiar—are familiar. Also the strange ones.

The midnight weeping behind a road's
roaring semis seems inconsolable.
On your way for lumber, listen
as others listened while hauling hides
to the French. Hear it as you go.

Lips

Hers are pursed to contain what
verges on speech, what might spill
into the air as a river slips from its banks.
The massed memory of upriver rain
and today's downpour push limbs,
leafy branches laden with tires,
a grocery cart, even a small suitcase
trailing kids' clothes. All turn
and grind like a hum shaping a word.
Now, it says, *now* beyond doubt,
beyond faith and berm and throat lump.
The torrent covers the ball field, licks
at the mound, fills the paved lot
to the latches of the sad, deserted cars.
Now, moans the river, *I will speak.*

Detritus

The wind flicks papers, shingles, sand
—blades slashing all—as we detach
what little siding scrappers hadn't
stripped long before Gloria
drank herself past waking. Her cats
and feral yard had pissed off
the kindest of us. We pry planks,
knock loose plaster and lath,
rip out doorframes and half the studs,
then drag all to a dumpster. Alongside
we stack branches from the dead ash.
The wind tears at our eyes,
screaming through opened walls
as a tall kid loops a rope over a beam.
Ragged neighbors fearing another shell,
its drunks, drugs, and inevitable flames,
we straighten our backs to squint,
seeing again our mix of garden plots
and sagging homes, feeling bloodflow
return to tired limbs. We line up,
cheer each other and pull the rope.

Tangle

I woke from surgery, words running to my lips.
One paused at the verge and all behind collided,
fell into a tangle of phonemes. So frames
of dreams collapse years of my life,

permit me to chase my toddlers and then
theirs through corridors and streets
of childhood. The images promise import
but slip loose from sense on waking; tales,

if they come, hum below morning noise
like words of a guy on a jackhammer
or the last forgetful phrase of a woman

fighting for breath. Breezes over a firepit
may suck from embers no flame but a glow
that shifts, brims, gleams as if to speak.

Scale

I google an allusion in a title and end up
reading about the Trojan War and feeling smart
or else the strain of becoming smart.
Then I'm ready to begin. In his first lines
the author alludes to the weight of the earth.
He's drawn a great scale of things heavy and light—
a certain woman's forgotten scarf (silk),
a skirt's scalloped hem, and the ashes
of his own body carried in a box on a bright day
in the future. I check his figures and find
his balance absurd. The earth weighs
6.58 sextillion tons.
How to weigh only the hem of a skirt?
A wool skirt could have some heft,
but this one might be silk like the scarf,
which can hardly be weighed, being lost.
The ashes should be straightforward, but
his container bothers me. Will it be maple
(closing with the rich click of a jewel box
to gleam on some well-appointed mantle)
or rough-sawn cedar, ready for a hole
under a tree? He's left this out. And how
big of a man is he? Are we to picture Keats'
frame reduced to chunks of bone and cinders,
or is he a big glowering sort, with heavy brows
and large hands batting the air as he reads?
I find him via the web and estimate.
He holds a girl in one image—perhaps
a grandchild, dressed for Christmas. Even
unburnt, the whole lot won't budge the scale.

Barn

Say one door of an old barn gets blown off
and just lies in the mud so goats and cows
would walk over it until the door was crushed
into cellulosic muck except there are no cows
and no farm because farming has broken more folks
than even poetry. So the wind whips through this
empty barn, bringing in snow and leaves in turn
—always a bit of what's going by. A family
stays here now and then, dodging Immigration
or the cold, the woman looking at her sleeping guy
and wondering if she was a fool to stay with him
after so much bullshit only to end up freezing
to death in a place like this. Often, of course,
it's empty, with only a faint creak of beams
answering the wind and relentless sun. Light
plays through the ragged roof and the grain
of the barnwood opens a bit more each year
so planks look sometimes like a map and
some days a face too old and tired to speak.

Descent

As flaps grind into place, wheels clunk down,
passengers turn from novels. Serious men
slide laptops into cases or fold papers.
The prattle of strangers fades as quiet
settles over those who rushed through gates

and groused at metal detectors, who will soon
grapple for bags and drive toward homes
and dinners, toward whatever makes us run.
All soften for a moment, submissive as dogs,
watching the tarmac lights rise through dusk.

In this lull, we forget for a time our hard looks,
the practiced flair, and lapse into what, here,
passes for contemplation. An odd law
of physics holds sway. Do we gray a bit?
Might a wrinkle escape our makeup?

Descending for so long, we recall our kids,
grown away from us in new cities and
new lives. Our lies, so tiny in the day's
fluorescence, loom now like the flat strip
below—large, bright, and imminent.

The descent slows and the plane slows,
but the moving earth signals speed
as trees and homes whip past and
wheels screech into our hearts
as everything near accelerates.

Detroit Mnemonic

Like refugees, we forget
by force. Whole cities vanish,
block by block; jobs go undone
that kept folks alive. Schoolkids
climb from rusted vans and wave

to bleary parents who may
never work again. A gaunt man
slips past in the 7-Eleven
unable to buy a slice with what
he got for scrounged bottles.

Churlish clerk, why not
just feed this mute?
I follow his gray shape
across the lot until I lose him
behind a hedge, trailing smoke,

face twisted away, clutching
tiny sausages in a greasy bag.
Poetry, this is not. Nor
opera, theatre, or even,
apparently, news. Yet a wind

raving through maples recalls
our old elms—those titans
that laced top branches
over the streets of childhood
and, when I fell in chase

or flight, held me

gaping into the strung web
of all things. No more.
Our hungry discards don't
mass at Ford's gates

facing Bennett's goons,
demanding work and bread.
Our grief only tangles traffic,
clutters parks, and seems
in the bright day quite mad.

Face

When he called her a bitch, I went for him,
wishing, of course, she hadn't added
her scolding to my words when he and
his pals scuffed my truck with a rock.
It's not like I knew what I'd do, being old
and never much of a fighter anyhow.
No one wins such stupidity, but I
kept moving just the same. Even sober,
my father would have barreled for them,
with some switch flipped behind his eyes.
Long dead, he wasn't dragging me
up the berm to their spot on the tracks.
I'm the man who carried my fist.
Somehow words leapt up and worked
an uneasy magic, as the mouthy guy
squinted, furled his lips. Down
the far side of the weedy slope, they slid
into the void that lay between school
and unemployment, having saved perhaps
a bit of face by spitting one last curse.

Stoplight

When he saw them on the grass by the on-ramp,
she was down and they were kicking her.
For some reason, he yanked his truck across
traffic and jumped out to scream at them
while Angelo shrank behind the dash and yelled,
"Goddammit, Bulletproof, get back inside!"
He heard tenderness in his partner's voice,
watched her dealers glare, point, and leave

as she struggled to rise and stagger off,
dazed, drugged, and weirdly barefoot—beheld
and forgotten by a hundred stalled commuters.
Then Angelo again and car horns chiming in,
so he slid back down—wanting to not know
where she'd go now—behind the wheel.

Phone Booths

Shouting details of love into cicadas clipped
to their ears and also into the campus bookstore
coffee shop or texting from a lecture hall as though
they have slipped into a momentary patch of fog
which shrouds them from a prof—kids don't
know the charm of plexiglass, steamed, scarred,
the aluminum frame, the maimed phone book,
names and numbers etched on every surface
but all unseen because this bubble in the world
is making her phone ring (you begging *pick up*
pick up) because panic has ripped the dial
of the indestructible black box and breathed
into the mouthpiece like it's Lester's last reed,
like it doesn't carry germ descendants from
the Spanish flu epidemic, which it probably does,
and when she picks up her end and starts
to forgive you, you know, across miles of wire,
under birds and squirrels through the worst night
of your short life, that she hears your voice
over the drunk pleading through the bifold,
the traffic screeching at the light, and the scream
that made you jump straight out of a nightmare
and land running to call before it was too late.

Watching Basie

For Deborah

On the tape, he spoke of Fats
and old K. C. His hair had yielded half
its great globe, but his hands
still made the late hour jump.

Your soft brows, perched
glasses, and delicate nose—how long
I have watched light flick
through the frame of your face,
as if fire could keep time.

When you found me I was broke
and, according to photographs,
in need of a razor. I had a sweet
baby, a rusted car, and parts
of a degree. Mad for you, I
bondoed myself into a man

I hoped you'd keep. Last night
you slept beside your mother,
holding her hand, stroking her hair.
I dozed on the couch as
Bill Evans eased our dreams.

One snowy night, a life ago,
I carried you down the street
on my back. We laughed as we
loved then, scraping deep
into our bellies. We heard

the downtown joints pulse
and burn all night, until our ears
rang with it, until it sang in our veins
when we held each other, when we
rocked our kids and then their kids.

On the tape, he spoke of Fats
and played breakneck stride. I watch
you soak it in to store with all
the old nights downtown, with what
comes into you in tunes and
comes out in touch.

Interferometry in Hell

Now we find dim planets with a trick:
mirrors tuned to cancel out wavelengths
of the star. How Zenlike the astronomer
who makes *aster* vanish like a smooth
center fielder blocking the sun with his glove
to find the small orb, its turning seams.

I recall that "pure serene" from my perch
in the mall where I wait for bifocals.
Lurid signs offer designer frames.
Waifish girls below CNN screens
spritz one and all with musk.

I dump *Science* for *The Inferno*
and descend through circles of the numb
and the cruel, relearning familiar sin,
familiar grief. From all earth's
corners, satellites beam blood,
spread like chips and cheese,
to America's sofas and my aging eyes.
Near some distant star, life percolates
on the skin of a dim, teeming ball.
Here, we are learning how to squint.

Habit

Outside the bar she hands a bill
to an old man. He's drunk
and says little, but she's gone
quick anyway and it's done
almost without thought, an act
leaking out like olive oil
from a cask, like sweat
from the bald trumpet player,
as he opens his spit valve
and shakes the horn, smiling
at a kid sitting in on bass,
as if to say, *It's OK—
you're not as bad as you
think. No one is.* Outside
the old man's drowsing again,
having given up the line of chat
he was making before a sweet
girl squeezed a ten into his hand
—her light, smooth touch—
one corner of the dry bill still
sticking up between fingers, a line
from the horn sliding past the noise
in the bar to him on the step and
to anyone just now walking past.

Cana Dance

after a play by Dario Fo

Not the idea of wine, but silken red,
sloshing goblets of it, jars, urns,
decanters, uncorked bottles of Fat
Bastard, pinot noir, Beaujolais, merlot,
even a cheap zinfandel for the groom's
grandmother, who sits watching
the riot unfold and perhaps thinks
of a long ago bed. Who wants

the idea of love? Blood in veins
counts and sweat beading on lips.
So we swarm the floor, shaking all
over as if each blown breath
might be our last—we who
drain our cups and live on earth.

Late on Her Birthday

The light that left the sun just over eight
minutes ago flares now in your hair, rings
your face, and floats above my Scotch.

Years ago, on a hillside where the river *is*
whiskey, a man dreaming liquid smoke
sealed an unblended cask. Some decades

back, your grandfather outlived strikes
in Colorado mines to marry, run a store,
and read the papers while he rocked you quiet.
Dead at fifty-nine, he was your first loss.

You speak of him as you drift off
holding my hand. While the light turns
and turns again, I hold your words, watch
the sky's last splash, and drain the glass.

Black Dog

Up late in search of calm,
I let the dog roam the pines
along the railroad. She flits
in and out of what little light
spills from the truck lot.
The faint clink of her collar dies
and she fades utterly away.
While I stare into nothing, she
moves through a cosmos of scent.

Above, where Andromeda should be,
at the edge of the visible,
the night is obscured by clouds
and glare. Some smart insomniac
at Palomar points a lens into dark
distance, chasing specks of life
a million light-years off.
Our hearts keep time, wend
without cease into worlds.

Short Stay Unit

So . . . the "record of wrongs"
that love doesn't keep is kept
quite well on nursing charts

though tears aren't totaled
beside the volume of urine,
the weight of a dormant man
in 12B (closed head trauma
and nowhere to go). His day's
claim on a bed is a second fall,

his only hope, one quick
woman who loses the trail
of his numbers for the one
instant that he retains,

who chides him awake and
bathes him like a child.

Repair

I feel for a wrench, then cramp up
and climb stairs to stretch under the murk
that floats above Detroit like a sky,

that tries to ride out our losses
—kids again killed in a drive-by
and waked by mourners rending the gray.

From here, I can make out the back
of an old church, where a sodden line
stretches down the alley. A bald guy

still shows up there to make soup
every damn day with a strange crew
of kids and grayheads crowding inside

to work amid pots of simmering beans,
as in a vast unacknowledged embrace.

Invisible Satellites

. . . daylight's invisible satellites, shamelessly
bouncing back from space the emptiness we feed them.
    Philip Booth

A boy on a tired road croaked
"Yo quiero tu agua." My hand lent
the bottle of tepid water and I went home,

safe under ancient orbs, under wads
of circuits that glow in high orbits and tug
on our weird human course. For backdrop,

I'd rather humors or the moon and stars
but no angels light the tale where kids
lug trash from the smoking dump, where

the earth heaves under shacks while a girl
is sold to cover debts. There the world
ends though it spins softly here while I sip

coffee, grade papers, and desire. *Yo quiero.*
Que quiero? What longing flits through
as though "bouncing back from space"

in vacuous waves of greed? On a road,
a child still scratches words in dust,
still measures and finds me wanting.

Feathers on a Dark Campus

Driven snow flashes through cones of light
along the walking paths. Girls in hoodies and parkas,
hunched boys pass. All lug packs of books and flakes

of circuitry.   Earlier, between blizzards,
I watched a cardinal flare to the bare top of a maple.
Where now, this paraclete?

                              Snow blasted,
they plod to class, unpack their bundles, pry
open books, and boot-up. They flirt or take notes.

Older than humans, the feather once
adorned the great reptiles. So say the fossils,
I intone. They click out "fossil."

Once, after getting beaten up, I rode a city bus,
watching my swollen reflection in sooty glass.
Neon storefronts blazed by, as the bus wheezed.

Caught on the wrong corner, I had taken a punch
and a few kicks, a scrawny kid in a dark
distant winter. How quickly youth lost

all those aches. They zip back into coats
and trudge toward cars and dorms. Snow
and the large dark swallow them so fast,

I wonder if I have only dreamt them,
pierced and dyed, into my empty desks.

Six Times

What a number of things you haven't seen
in this street you travel six times a day.
      Paul Valéry

An angle of light carves a trellis
crusted by snow, flecked by leaves.

A snap of wind tears the maples,
shouting, North—north!

Buffeted, my half-dressed students
bound through the campus.

One lags, frail. I watch the wind. Once,

I saw my young wife, her gait gone
wooden, leave the last wounds

of her clinic and step
into the light of an old day.

Dad and I, in a Snap

For Kathy

In an embrace or a tackle
you grasped your helmeted child
turned toward the daughter who held the camera
who would sticker it into an album for me,
who would soon, when we lost the house
and pictured yard, not speak a word to you
for months, then learn to pity and forgive.

With a smile—as you verged
on such loss—or a grimace,
bending an athlete's soul
over an alcoholic belly
(where are the war hero,
the semi-pro catcher you were?)

and looking into this last flick
of bright sobriety, you held a boy
in a blue jersey who would watch
the manhood seep from you,
who would shun your beloved army
but carry with him everywhere
your pocketknife rage and love.

Sunlight

All it is is sunlight on granite.
        Robert Hass, *"Breach and Orison"*

The indignity of being just a man
going west in a freight car,
freezing, fleeing luck or debt—
or maybe doing seventy-five
in a four-wheel pop can
chasing what might be a job —
and needing most to take a piss
and then to sleep for days.
And from the train my dad
didn't take because the war
took him or from my Honda,
we watch light linger on a rock
face as though the sun has done
its bit just for us. Some night,
decades apart, we'll walk
into our homes, each of us,
to find our wives have dressed,
have gotten the kids stowed
somehow, have put on rouge,
and, like this dusk, it'll be
more right than ever again—
at least for my old man
since the war stole more
than its share. For me, such
days stretch out like cats
on a ledge in late summer
until the sun fades to black
and leaves no mark on the rock
when the long dark resumes.

Smoke

Blown from exhaust vents into the street,
a smell assembles itself of solvents
in air already carboned by cars

and car-making, by all that comes at last
from fire, even from cells
he coughs out as he passes the cleaners.

Among suits at her counter stood a woman
not old then—his own mother, alive
in ways unnamed in his boy's mind.

Memory assembles now upon nerves
and a late June day and the sag
of a much older boy: her bright face

before the end of work when shit wages
and a drab flat pulled on her skin like
time. She's buried now—ashes added

to her husband's grave, her dates carved.
Who, in years to come, will know
the laughing blaze that left this smoke?

Rain

Pummeling the deck, rain soaks into cedar grain,
piles into puddles, and blasts the puddles back
into light. I have wondered what old men think
staring into rain like this as though it refracts
the dull day and thickens the air so that bits
of the past coalesce and shine like a film
shown through mist on some old brick facade.
Maybe old women and men are looking out of doors
for all the gray miles of this storm, each
exhaling a puff of one cloud—the one roof
we all share. This rain, insistent and slow,
falls for hours to save our plants, to chase
kids home from a ballgame, to give
lovers a beat to match the pulse, and to house
for a day all those who have really left us.

Entering America After Driving All Night

Alert, packing serious heat, the guard
lacks only irony when he asks
the purpose of my trip. *A conference,*
I mutter, bleary from roads trailing back
through Ontario to New England like a chain
of caffeine phantasms broken by semis,
white lines, and rumble strips.
What kind, he wants to know.
Poetry, I offer, certain that no one
would invent this lie. He has me pop
the trunk to launch a muffled search
for off-rhymes, *Asian Figures,* or
nonce sonnets gone bad.

It is late, my muscular friend.
Really, it was late and has become
early again, but I crave the end
of a dream born a hundred miles back.
Threats lurk about us, discreet
as Pinsky's voice, as sex in Frost's woods,
the pathos of persona poems—as
all my rambling texts scanned
in the weird light of customs hell.
The right thing in the wrong place
is what we seek. Unlikely and indefensible
Truth has offered itself again
and been found wanting.

After Mourning

For Jesse

Like acid, his life washes over you,
cutting you again, flaring the old welts
but erasing at last that flinch you learned
sharing a room and dodging blows,
that hitch in your voice retuned
each year by a well-tooled jab.
Those old burrs are sluiced off
to the sewers and gone. Your blues
pours out now and, around you, time
bubbles up like a beat that calls
now and now and now. Like you,
your brother is all of his ages at once
though, dead this time and not drunk,
his parts will make no sum. Alive,
you step again onto the new asphalt
of an old street, dribbling a ball
and looking for a game. Sing out
for us. We'll leap from our stoops.